Respect the Work
Republishing Books in the Public Domain

Barbara A. B. Seiders, Ph.D.

Dedication

Thanks, McQ, for bringing the "Anne Does Green Gables" brouhaha to my attention. Your disappointment at the poorly chosen cover image for the well-loved character made me glad that I had gone to such great lengths to reproduce *The Corner Stone* by Margaret Hill McCarter as faithfully as I was able. The heated reaction to the poor choice of that publisher made me realize that the choices we make as readers (and for me as a new publisher) are important, that it is appropriate that we honor original authors of creative works.

Preface

I left a career of thirty years in national security technology and policy, and decided to indulge my passion for facilitating successful leadership and team building as a writer emphasizing those topics. I looked forward to evaluating self-publishing as a means to distribute materials on those subjects. When I found a copy of the 1915 book *The Corner Stone* by Margaret Hill McCarter, the prospect of restoring the book and making it available by republication seemed a reasonable strategy to learn more about the process of self-publishing. As a tiny, newly fledged publisher, I invested many hours in learning about copyright protection, public domain works, capturing text for preparation of published materials, and the process of actually making the work available for others through Amazon. I painstakingly edited text from an imperfect OCR processor, and became fluent in Photoshop™ as I prepared a fresh version of the original artwork. I immersed myself in research about the author, the illustrator, the times in which they lived, the times in which the story was set, as well as the history – and geography – of Kansas in the early days of settlement. When I finished, I felt that the newly published edition of *The Corner Stone (Annotated)* would have made Margaret McCarter proud.

Once I made the book available from Amazon, I began to see more and more copies of books from the same era that were poorly reproduced, for which publishers were charging exorbitant prices. The more of these I saw, the more important it became to me to advocate for publications of public domain works whose quality reflected a level of respect for the author of the original creative endeavor.

And then I saw a discussion about an edition of *Anne of Green Gables* in which a self-publisher selected a particularly poor cover image for the well-loved book. The reaction to the poor quality of publication motivated me to capture my thoughts on the question of republishing the work of others, and I posted three articles on the subject to the blog on my webpage. Subsequently, I gathered up those posts in this small book, edited them, added more detail and a discussion of my efforts on *The Corner Stone*. My goal in this little book is to encourage both publishers and readers to ... *Respect the Work.*

Barbara A. B. Seiders
One Hundred Year Horizons

Contents

1 Respect the Work

If there were a code of ethics for publishers who republish the works of others, it could begin with the provision paraphrased from the Hippocratic Oath, "Do no harm". At a minimum, those who intend to publish the works of others, particularly those who seek to profit from such publication, should ensure that their publication does not detract from the original. Far better if publishers of materials in the public domain honor the original author of the work with a publication whose quality demonstrates respect for the original creative effort.

What does it mean for a publisher to demonstrate respect for the original author of a public domain work? The following are representative of the things that a respectful publisher will do when making public domain work available in a new edition.

- Ensure that the work is in fact in the public domain, and is not protected by copyright.
- Provide a quality rendering of the work, including cover imagery or interior illustrations, consistent with the context of the original work.
- Reproduce the work accurately and completely.
- Ensure reproduction does not detract from the original work.
- Make the work accessible to a wider audience than in its original form and distribution.
- Provide context that supports the original creative work.

The following chapters describe examples of choices by publishers in reproducing public domain works that reflect poorly on the originals. These choices include examples of poor cover images, bad rendering of the text, incomplete reproductions, and possibly illegal production of works still protected by copyright. The examples are drawn largely from publications of *Anne of Green Gables* by Lucy Maud Montgomery, in response to a controversy that occurred when a publisher chose a particularly bad cover image to represent the beloved character, Anne Shirley.

Examples of publication choices are also provided – both positive and negative – from productions of *The Corner Stone* by Margaret Hill McCarter. *The Corner Stone* was the first republication undertaken by One Hundred Year Horizons. Having invested time and resources to produce a quality publication for print and electronic readers, it is discouraging to see "books" offered for sale, sometimes at exorbitant prices, of poor quality showing little respect for the original author.

Readers who value the creative endeavor that results in a book worth reading can encourage publishers to treat the works of original authors with respect. Specifically, readers can:

- Endeavor not to buy (or download illegally) books that violate copyright;
- Let publishers know that poor quality editions are unacceptable;
- Avoid buying "books" produced using automated shortcuts;
- Support publishers who invest in quality publications of public domain works; and
- Support publishers whose imprints demonstrate respect for the original authors of creative works.

Respect the Work was written to offer illustrations of the differences in production choices, and to encourage readers to make better informed choices when seeking out public domain republications. Specifically, readers who respect an author's creative endeavor should either support services such as Project Gutenberg that make public domain books freely available, or publishers who invest in producing quality reproductions of others' original creative work.

2 Republishing Public Domain Works

2.1 The Process

The process of capturing a creative work in the public domain and reproducing it for sale is not difficult, and can be largely automated. The quality of the resulting publication is determined by the extent to which the publisher invests in producing a product that respects the work of the original author. Not all publishers do. In the interest of profiting from the work of others, some publishers make poor choices and take shortcuts in producing new editions of existing works that show little respect for the original author of the creative work.

The availability of self-publishing services offers the exciting opportunity to recapture books out of print, to be enjoyed again by contemporary readers. For works that are in the public domain, there are a number of means available to capture the text and rapidly re-publish the work. Amazon, a driving force in the emergence of self-publishing, provides Kindle Direct Publishing (KDP) [1] for their Kindle series of electronic readers, and CreateSpace (CS) [2] for hard-copy publishing. There are other similar resources for production, marketing and sales of self-published works available for other booksellers and platforms. The examples described here derive from the Amazon services, as that is where the controversy first arose.

The steps needed to capture a public domain work and publish it on KDP or CS are: 1) capture the text, 2) format the book, 3) compile using services provided by KDP and CS, 4) decide on pricing and distribution, and 5) publish! The Amazon services offer help, recommendations and templates for every step of the process. You can add a specially designed cover for your republished book, or choose one of the templates or generic versions offered by KDP and CS. The entire process can be somewhat time consuming depending on the care taken in capturing the work or designing the format, but it is straightforward, and ultimately not very difficult.

Amazon does have policies in place with the goal to provide a positive experience for the reader who buys books at Amazon.com. One of these policies is that if a publisher is going to publish a public domain work, they should add value to it. Adding literary commentary, historical context of the period, or new illustrations or maps, all constitute adding value to a public domain work. It is still possible to republish work without annotating or prefacing it, but if Amazon chooses to publish the work itself, it will eliminate the catalog postings for undifferentiated versions.

2.2 In Which We Meet Anne, of Green Gables

Anne Shirley is the well-loved character in a series of stories by author Lucy Maud Montgomery, the first of which is *Anne of Green Gables*. The reader first meets Anne when Montgomery introduces her as

> *A child of about eleven, garbed in a very short, tight, very ugly dress of yellowish-gray wincey. She wore a faded brown sailor hat and beneath the hat, extending down her back, were two braids of very thick, decidedly red hair.*

Throughout the stories, in which she ages from a young girl of eleven to a young woman, Anne is characterized by her "decidedly" red hair, freckles, good heart and active imagination.

Copyright protection on most of the stories in the series has lapsed. As a result, publishers are able to reproduce the stories and offer them for sale. Someone looking to buy a copy of *Anne of Green Gables* from Amazon.com would first see the cover images selected by republishers of the story.

Searching Amazon.com for a well-loved book such as *Anne of Green Gables* is an excellent way to see the variety of approaches that publishers take in presenting an existing work in a new publication. In the first two front covers (Figure 1 [3] and Figure 2 [4]), the publishers have used similarly iconic images, clearly associated with Anne, but with very different graphic art styles and degrees of artistic sophistication. [N.B. The image shown in Figure 2 was the cover image as of February, 2013; the image was changed sometime after that and as of March 2013 now features a pose with the same model as other editions, see Figure 6 and Figure 7.] In the third example (Figure 3 [5]), the publisher has used a photograph which is more subtly, indirectly associated with Anne and her "decidedly red hair".

Figure 1 Anne of Green Gables Cover Illustration 1 (left)

Figure 2 Anne of Green Gables Cover Illustration 2 (right)

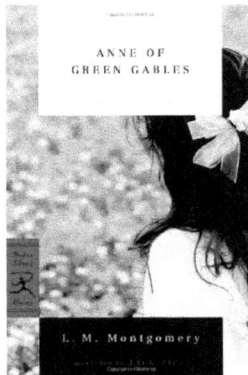

Figure 3 Anne of Green Gables Cover Illustration 3

Finding an image that suits the book can be difficult. The examples shown in Figure 4 [6] and Figure 5 [7] illustrate alternative approaches taken by publishers. In Figure 4, the publisher has chosen a photograph suggestive of the era when the story takes place. In the course of the specific story, *Anne of Green Gables*, Anne ages from 11 to about 16. The image selected may be a stretch in depicting a girl of 16, but it is not unreasonable. As an image of Anne, however, it suffers from lack of anything resembling her distinctive braids. Another approach to selecting a cover for a book to be republished is to use a photograph of the author, as in Figure 5, covering a compilation of works by Lucy Maud Montgomery, including *Anne of Green Gables*. Using a picture of the author eliminates any negative associations between the image and the story within, but it may also diminish the connection that the reader has to the characters.

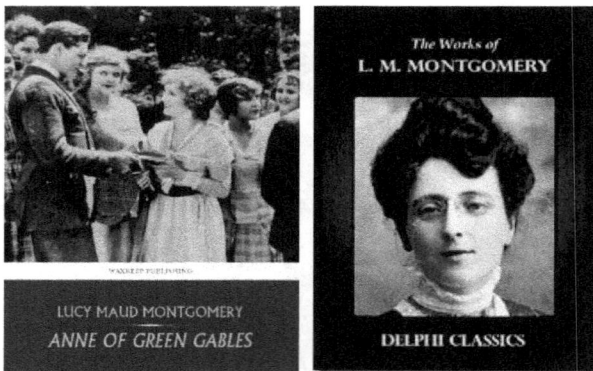

Figure 4 Anne of Green Gables Cover Illustration 4 (left)

Figure 5 Anne of Green Gables Cover Illustration 5 (right)

For their cover of *Anne of Green Gables*, Simon and Brown Publishers selected a stock photograph [8] for the cover that shows a lovely young woman, in period dress, with a hint of braid, barely visible, caught up in her unmistakably red hair (Figure 6 [9]). In the story, Anne ages to 16 years. The image selected by Simon and Brown is lovely, but the young woman in the image is clearly older than 16, making the use of the image by Simon and Brown specifically for *Anne of Green Gables* less than ideal.

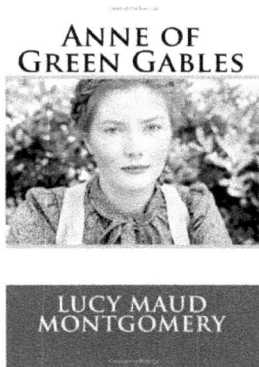

Figure 6 Anne of Green Gables Cover Illustration 6 (left)

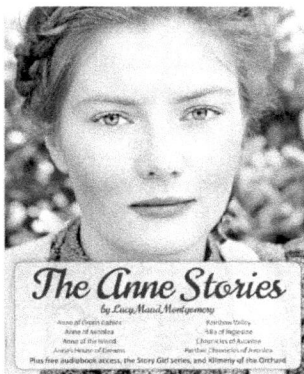

Figure 7 Anne of Green Gables Cover Illustration 7 (right)

Aside from the issue of being an appropriate age for *Anne of Green Gables* specifically, the model selected in the image published by Simon and Brown is generally well suited to Anne, the character. Therefore, it is not surprising to find the same image also featured in another edition (Figure 7 [10]). Aaron Kerr compiled a collection of stories under the title "*The Anne Stories*". Clearly familiar with and fond of the main character, Kerr cites his reason for publishing the collection in the product description:

> *As the father of four daughters who LOVE the Anne books, I set out to create the ultimate Kindle edition of these timeless books. I wanted a perfectly-formatted, easy-to-use Kindle release at a price that couldn't be beat.*

In the stories compiled by Kerr, Anne ages from 11 to adulthood. Under these circumstances, the image selected by Kerr is appropriate to the span of the story. In the Kerr edition, the photograph has been modified to add a sprinkle of faintly visible freckles. The freckles also feature prominently in the story, adding to the authenticity of the association between the cover image and the story.

Each of the examples shown so far is, within the bounds of artistic license, reasonably appropriate for use as a cover for a republication of *Anne of Green Gables*. In contrast, the cover chosen by an independent publisher using the CreateSpace publishing platform (Figure 8 [11]), represents an image choice that is wholly at odds with the character as created by the author and portrayed in the book.

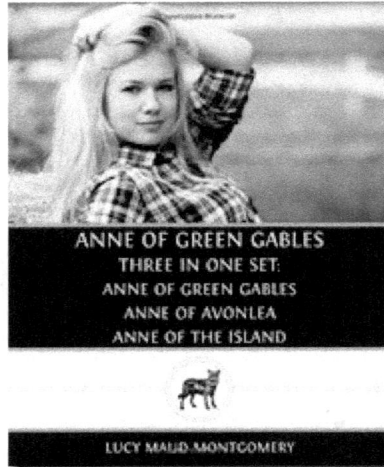

Figure 8 Anne of Green Gables Cover Illustration 8

As with the Kerr compilation, the CreateSpace publisher included stories in which Anne ages from 11 to young adulthood. Therefore, selection of a model who could represent Anne at the end of the series is reasonable and acceptable. However, two things make this choice of image inappropriate for the cover of the stories of Anne Shirley. First, the model has blond hair, and plainly does not represent a character with "decidedly red hair". If a character's hair color were inconsequential to the telling of a story, making an artistic change like this might be acceptable. In this case, however, the image of Anne with her flame red hair in braids is an important part of who Anne is, and the choice of a model with a different hair color demonstrates a lack of familiarity with -- and respect for -- the work being republished. The second issue with this choice of cover image has to do with the atmosphere of the stories written by L. M. Montgomery. Anne of Green Gables is smart, sweet and innocent, a positive role model for young girls. The image chosen in Figure 8 reflects a more sexualized character that is inconsistent with the Anne as created by Montgomery.

When the book was advertised on Amazon.com, it generated a fierce backlash among loyal readers of the *Anne of Green Gables* stories. CreateSpace quickly removed the image, and listed the book as "Temporarily out of stock". The speed, volume and energy of the reaction from readers reflected on Amazon product reviews and on social networks should send a clear message to publishers looking to republish works in the public domain: respect the work, and offer a product that honors the original author with an authentic, faithful reproduction of their creation.

3   Shortcuts Used to Republish Public Domain Works

The controversy over the cover image for *Anne of Green Gables* should serve to encourage those who republish materials in the public domain to honor the original author with an authentic, faithful reproduction of their work.

I first learned about the *Anne of Green Gables* controversy when a friend posted a link to the article in the Guardian [12] on his Facebook timeline. His post was scathing, and his friends visibly disappointed and angry in their comments. Their reaction to what had been done to the image of the character of Anne was comparable to what I might expect if they were talking about a close friend in real life whose image and character had been maligned. The intensity of their reaction was also reflected by commenters in the reviews [13] left for the edition on Amazon.com.

This energetic reaction to a poor cover image for a story originally published in 1908 should serve as fair warning to publishers who elect to republish materials in the public domain: readers care. Capturing historic creative works so that they can be enjoyed now and in the future is a worthwhile enterprise. When public domain books are made available for free, as from Project Gutenberg [14] providing them in easily produced formats is understandable and acceptable. But if a publisher charges for an edition that would otherwise be available in the public domain, they should add value to the work, or at least not detract from it, as was the case of the poor cover choice for *Anne of Green Gables*.

A poor quality cover design unsuitable to the work is perhaps the most visible indication that a publisher is not respectful of the work of original authors. Additional short cuts that publishers take that reflect poorly on the original author involve capturing and reproducing text and graphics. Two common means of capturing text from a public domain work are capturing the text as an image of the page, and scanning the document and processing it with optical character recognition (OCR) software.

3.1 Compiling Page Images as Books

Publishers sometimes offer as books compilations of images of the pages from the original work, bound electronically or physically. If the book were composed of reproductions of major works of art, high quality illustration plates, or ornate calligraphy, a book consisting of bound page images might be warranted as the best means to make the work available to contemporary readers. Aside from unique cases such as these, copying and compiling page images most often results in a poor quality book. When the pages are imaged, compiled, and bound into a physical volume, often the text quality is poor to begin with and made even worse in the course of reproduction. If the image is recorded strictly as a high-contrast, low-resolution, black-and-white document image, illustrations in light-colored ink may be washed out altogether.

The snips below (Figure 9) illustrate these differences. The snip on the left was taken from an edition of Margaret Hill McCarter's *The Corner Stone*, provided in electronic portable document format (pdf) for free from Forgotten Books [15]. The snip on the right is a high resolution color scan from an original paperback copy of the book. To begin, comparing the two snips shows the degradation in text quality as a result of the low resolution scanning process to produce the pdf edition on the left. Second, in the Forgotten Books edition, the first word, with drop cap formatting, has been lost. This loss is only one word out of sixty, or less than 2% of the text, but it makes reading and understanding the passage incrementally more difficult. Finally, in capturing the text as a high-contrast, black-and-white document, the two lines of golden graphics the original publisher used to set off the text passage have been lost altogether.

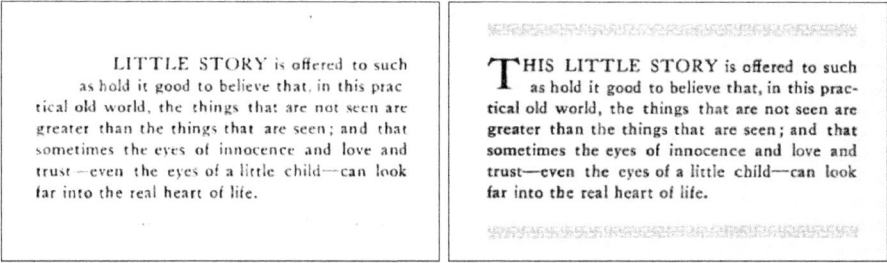

LITTLE STORY is offered to such as hold it good to believe that, in this practical old world, the things that are not seen are greater than the things that are seen; and that sometimes the eyes of innocence and love and trust—even the eyes of a little child—can look far into the real heart of life.

THIS LITTLE STORY is offered to such as hold it good to believe that, in this practical old world, the things that are not seen are greater than the things that are seen; and that sometimes the eyes of innocence and love and trust—even the eyes of a little child—can look far into the real heart of life.

Figure 9 Comparison of text image capture quality

In addition to poor text quality from the original scan, a book composed of page images has other disadvantages. Image compression used to format the page for an electronic reader can reduce the image quality even further. Also, since the pages consist of a single image, it is not possible to manipulate the font choice, font size, or other features available on electronic readers. Finally, easy navigation within the text of a book and the ability to search for words and phrases are two benefits provided by electronic readers. When publishers offer a book composed of page images for reading on electronic readers, the book rarely includes an active table of contents or index, or the ability to search the text.

One publisher extends the caveat below for historic books that they offer produced as compiled page images:

> *This is a reproduction of a book published before 1923. This book may have occasional imperfections such as missing or blurred pages, poor pictures, errant marks, etc. that were either part of the original artifact, or were introduced by the scanning process. We believe this work is culturally important, and despite the imperfections, have elected to bring it back into print as part of our continuing commitment to the preservation of printed works worldwide. We appreciate your understanding of the imperfections in the preservation process, and hope you enjoy this valuable book.*

Another publisher provides this caveat:

> *[This publisher] utilizes the latest technology to regenerate facsimiles of historically important writings. Careful attention has been made to accurately preserve the original format of each page whilst digitally enhancing the aged text.*

At least the reader of these books has been informed what to expect.

3.2 Compiling Unedited OCR Processed Pages as Books

The second method used to capture text from existing manuscripts for republication is to scan the document and process the text using optical character recognition (OCR). There are numerous programs that can be used for OCR processing that rapidly convert a page image into editable text. The OCR will be subject to introducing errors if the page is dirty or damaged, if the font or kerning is too small, if the font in the original work is too ornate, or if the image text is badly aligned. Some OCR programs handle tables, columns and text boxes particularly badly, mixing the text together into a single line. Finally, OCR can introduce errors into punctuation, or more commonly, miss punctuation completely.

Processing a page image by OCR can provide as much as 90 – 95% of the document text, but it is exceedingly rare that any OCR program will generate a page with 100% accuracy and completeness. Eliminating errors that have been introduced into the text and ensuring that all of the text was captured requires editing, comparing the original to the OCR text, page by page, line by line, word by word. It can take longer to proofread and correct the processed text than it would take for an accomplished typist to enter the text from scratch.

To illustrate the need for proofreading text generated using OCR on a page image, the snip on the left below (Figure 10) is part of a page from an original copy of *The Corner Stone*. The snip on the right shows the result from using OCR on this image, without editing. There are nine errors in a selection of about 150 words, or 6% error rate. The OCR program used to process this passage was the best of the three programs used in capturing *The Corner Stone*.

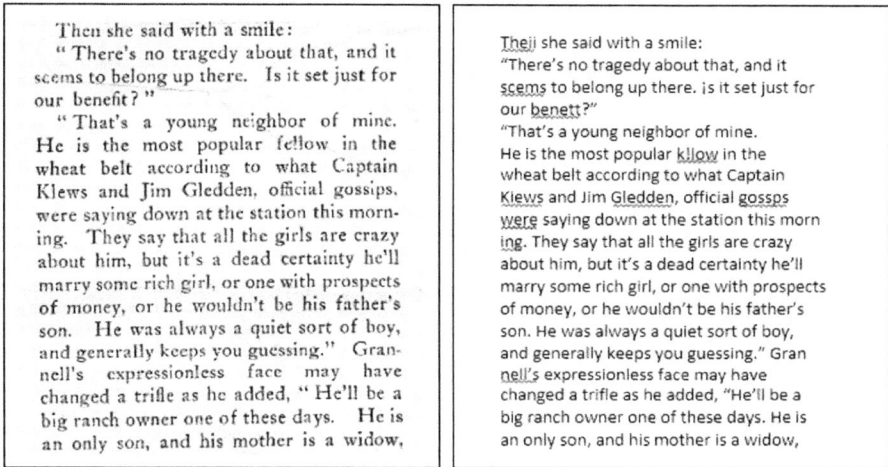

Then she said with a smile: " There's no tragedy about that, and it seems to belong up there. Is it set just for our benefit? " " That's a young neighbor of mine. He is the most popular fellow in the wheat belt according to what Captain Klews and Jim Gledden, official gossips, were saying down at the station this morning. They say that all the girls are crazy about him, but it's a dead certainty he'll marry some rich girl, or one with prospects of money, or he wouldn't be his father's son. He was always a quiet sort of boy, and generally keeps you guessing." Grannell's expressionless face may have changed a trifle as he added, " He'll be a big ranch owner one of these days. He is an only son, and his mother is a widow,	Theji she said with a smile: "There's no tragedy about that, and it scems to belong up there. is it set just for our benett?" "That's a young neighbor of mine. He is the most popular kllow in the wheat belt according to what Captain Kiews and Jim Gledden, official gossps were saying down at the station this morn ing. They say that all the girls are crazy about him, but it's a dead certainty he'll marry some rich girl, or one with prospects of money, or he wouldn't be his father's son. He was always a quiet sort of boy, and generally keeps you guessing." Gran nell's expressionless face may have changed a trifle as he added, "He'll be a big ranch owner one of these days. He is an only son, and his mother is a widow,

Figure 10 Comparison of original text and OCR capture

Scanning a book and converting the text using OCR can be completed entirely automatically. Unfortunately, not all publishers are willing to invest the time and labor required to proofread text obtained by OCR from a scanned image. Some publishers offer the raw, unedited text obtained by processing the image with OCR as an electronic book. An incomplete and inaccurate reproduction is far more disrespectful of an original creative work than is making a poor choice of cover design.

Recapturing a public domain work by processing the page image with OCR requires significant editing, but it also offers advantages over compiling page images, particularly with respect to publishing in electronic form. For a publisher who chooses to capture text from an original work using OCR, the resultant text is more amenable to formatting with section headings and tables of contents, and can be searched. The publisher can change the font used to present the text, and is not constrained to the font used in the original work. Once formatted for a particular brand of electronic reader, the font size – and in some cases even the choice of font – can be manipulated by the reader, making for an improved reading experience. These benefits, however, are not enough to overcome poorly edited text.

My friend was alarmed at the poor choice that a publisher made for the cover of a republication of a well-loved book; I find it egregious that publishers are able to profit from the creative work of others when their choices for how to capture and present that work ultimately detract from the original. As someone who buys both hard copy and electronic copy of historic works, I avoid publishers who take shortcuts such as those described here, and look for publishers who honor the original creative work with an authentic and faithful reproduction of that work.

The next chapter provides more detail on what it means that a publisher honors the original author.

4 Honor the Author with an Authentic Reproduction

In Chapter 2, I described aspects of the process of republishing works in the public domain. In Chapter 3, I described steps in the process in more detail, and in particular shortcuts taken by some publishers that result in such a poor quality book that it reflects disrespect on the author of the original creative work. This chapter addresses what can be done by publishers to encourage republication of editions of works in the public domain that honor the author of the original creative work.

4.1 Ensure that the work is in the public domain.

The first step in making a public domain work available by republication is to ensure that it is in fact in the public domain, and not still protected by copyright. Even if the author is long dead, the copyright protections on the author's work may be in place. Copyright law is complex, and protections afforded to a creative work vary depending on when (or if) it was published, when (or if) it was registered, where it may have been copyrighted, and when or whether an existing copyright on the work has been renewed.

There are resources available that provide guidance on what may be expected for determining copyright status. The U.S. Copyright Office [16] is a good place to start, with definitive data sources and helpful reference materials. Cornell University has an in-house Copyright Information Center [17] whose webpage includes valuable resources, including a summary table, "Copyright Term and the Public Domain in the United States" [18] that describes many of the dates and conditions that affect whether or not a work is in the public domain. In addition to determining whether the original work was copyrighted at the time of publication, it is necessary to determine whether an existing copyright has been renewed. Stanford University maintains a database of copyright renewals [19] and makes it publicly available. Querying Project Gutenberg_[14] can be helpful – if there is an undifferentiated edition of the work available on Project Gutenberg, it is likely that the work is in the public domain.

Even when a publisher is committed to due diligence, it can be difficult to determine the status of a given piece of work. For example, many of the compilations of the work of Lucy Maud Montgomery, author of *Anne of Green Gables* discussed in the prior posts, include the story *Anne of Windy Poplars*. *Anne of Windy Poplars* was originally published in Canada in 1936. By Canadian law [20],

> *Copyright in a work exists for the life of the author/creator, the remainder of the calendar year in which he is deceased, plus fifty years after the end of that calendar year.*

Montgomery passed away in 1942, so her works passed into public domain in 1993 — in Canada. Her stories were also copyrighted in the United States. The U.S. copyright was registered for *Anne of Windy Poplars* in 1936, and renewed in 1963 [21]. This presents an unusual situation in which the story is available in the public domain in Canada and elsewhere (e.g., Australia), but is (apparently) protected by copyright in the United States. The situation is further complicated by the availability of editions online. Copyright restrictions for electronic media apply at the location where the electronic version resides, that is, at the geographic location of the specific network server. The disposition of copyright protection on electronic versions makes for peculiar circumstances. *Anne of Windy Poplars* is available at Gutenberg Australia, where it has been determined to be in the public domain; it is not available at Project Gutenberg in the United States. Furthermore, the Gutenberg Australia version (maintained in the United States by an American) is accompanied by this warning [22]:

Warning! Restricted Access!

*The title you have selected (**Anne of Windy Poplars**) is a post-1922 publication by an author who died more than 50 years ago. Such titles are in the public domain in many countries, particularly those outside the US and Europe. However, this title most likely* **remains copyrighted** *under United States law, where works copyrighted in 1923 or later can remain under copyright for up to 95 years after publication. It may also be copyrighted in European Union countries and other countries where copyrights can last longer than 50 years past the author's death. (Europe, for instance, uses a life plus 70 years term.)* Follow this link [link disabled] *for more details on copyright laws of various countries. Below, we provide author death dates and other edition information, so that you can check this information against the terms of your country's copyright law.*

Do NOT download or read this book online if you or your system are in the United States*, or in another country where copyrights for authors with the dates shown below have not expired. The author's estate and publishers still retain rights to control distribution and use of the work in those countries.*

As a small, aspiring American publisher, I would not publish *Anne of Windy Poplars* under my imprint, either by itself or in compilation. I would also avoid making a copy available for Kindle, as Amazon Kindle servers fall under US copyright [23].

Determining whether the author, their estate, or their agent still hold copyright on an original work is the first step in honoring the original creator of the work.

4.2 *Provide a quality rendering of the work.*

The second step in honoring the author of an original creative work is to provide a quality rendering of the work. As discussed in Chapter 3, publishers sometimes choose to provide a "book" which is simply a bound compilation of page images scanned from a hard copy of the original work. There are books for which this might be appropriate – collections of fine art, or perhaps hand-penned works that will not render well by optical character recognition (OCR) programs and whose calligraphy is as much a part of the artistry as the text itself. For most volumes, however, building a book from page images makes for a poor quality "book". Surprisingly, in some cases, these compilations of page images are offered at a price that well exceeds what a traditionally formatted book would cost. A publisher who expects to profit by making someone else's creative work available for sale should make it available in a format that is worthy of the price.

4.3 Reproduce the work accurately and completely.

The third step in honoring an author by republishing their work is to reproduce it accurately and completely. As described in detail in Chapter 3, publishers commonly use OCR on scanned images of original work without proofreading or thoroughly editing the resulting text. This method can result in lost text, introduces errors into the reproduction, and does not reflect well on the original author — or the publisher. Recapturing the text purely for the sake of preserving the work may justify expedient methods; recapturing the text with the intent to profit from sale of the work should be undertaken with regard for an accurate and complete reproduction of the book.

4.4 Ensure reproduction does not detract from the work.

In Chapter 2, I described a particularly bad choice for cover illustration for a republication of *Anne of Green Gables* by Lucy Maud Montgomery. As Montgomery presented her, the character, Anne Shirley, was a sweet and innocent young girl with decidedly red hair. The choice of a blond and sexualized model for the cover made it obvious that the publisher was unfamiliar with the work that they sought to republish. The reaction in comments on Amazon.com from readers familiar with the beloved character was swift and fierce, and resulted in CreateSpace making the publication "Temporarily out of stock". Publishers who seek to profit from republication of the creative work of someone else should ensure that their editorial choices do not detract from the original work. As the *Anne of Green Gables* example illustrates, such choices demonstrate lack of respect for the author and her characters, and can result in damage to the reputation – and sales – of the publisher.

4.5   *Use technology to make the work more accessible.*

An accurate reproduction of a historic creative work should take into account the period in which it was first made available, as well as the era in which the work is set. This consideration extends to choice of fonts, especially when the text has been captured by a technique that permits choice of font.

As noted in Chapter 3 text which has been captured and processed by OCR can be displayed in fonts other than what was used originally, either by the publisher, or in some cases by the individual using their electronic reading device. Choice of fonts affects readers in different ways. The snip in Figure 11 shows the first few lines of *Anne of Green Gables* from Project Gutenberg in which the typeface has a modest serif. The same lines are shown in Figure 12 from Forgotten Books [24], in a sans serif typeface. Offering a book originally published in 1908 in a sans serif font seems inconsistent with the standards of the period, and may be unappealing to some readers from an aesthetic perspective. However, sans serif typeface may be easier to read for some people, particularly those are visually impaired or who are dyslexic [25]. In this case, having the ability for the publisher or the reader to present the text in the font which works best for them – from either a practical or aesthetic perspective - makes the work more accessible than it would have been in original form.

> ## CHAPTER I. Mrs. Rachel Lynde is Surprised
>
> Mrs. Rachel Lynde lived just where the Avonlea main road dipped down into a little hollow, fringed with alders and ladies' eardrops and traversed by a brook that had its source away back in the woods of the old Cuthbert place; it was reputed to be an

Figure 11 Serif font used by Project Gutenberg in Anne of Green Gables

> ### MRS. RACHEL LYNDE IS SURPRISED
>
> M RS. Rachel Lynde lived just where the Avonlea main road dipped down into a little hollow, fringed with alders and ladies' eardrops and traversed by a brook that had its source away back in the woods of the old Cuthbert place; it was reputed to be an intricate,

Figure 12 Sans serif font used by Forgotten Books in Anne of Green Gables

4.6 Provide context that supports the original work.

A particular advantage of being able to republish an original creative work is having the ability to enrich the work with information that would not have been available to the author at the time the book was written. A publisher can add historical context that gives modern readers a better appreciation for the events and attitudes of the era in which the book is set, and in which the author wrote. A story can be annotated with biographical information of the author subsequent to the publication of the work, including the effect of the author's work on events to come. Reference materials can be added, providing links, both literally and figuratively, between the creative work and its larger context.

5   Case Study: *The Corner Stone* by Margaret Hill McCarter

My reaction to the controversy over the poor reproduction of Lucy Maud Montgomery's *Anne of Green Gables* was a direct result of my own experience republishing a book that was in the public domain. That book is *The Corner Stone* by Margaret Hill McCarter, originally published in 1915. I found a copy of the book among my mother's belongings; nearly one hundred years old, it was in pretty sad condition (Figure 13). *The Corner Stone* is a sweet little romance, set in the early days of homesteading in Kansas.

When I found the book, I had recently left my job of nearly twenty years to take up writing and self-publishing in the area of leadership and teamwork. I thought that restoring the McCarter book would allow me to accomplish parallel goals: restore a book that was no longer readily available for contemporary readers, and learn about the process of self-publishing.

5.1   *Evaluating Copyright Status*

My first step was to determine whether McCarter's *The Corner Stone* was still protected by copyright. I reviewed copyright law, and evaluated the term of the existing copyright, and determined that unless someone had renewed the copyright, it was unlikely to be protected by copyright. I reviewed the database of copyright renewals; I could find no record of a renewal. I looked for copies of the title on Project Gutenberg; there were none. I found other copies of the book available for sale, undifferentiated, and so concluded that it was unlikely to be protected by copyright.

Figure 13 Original copy of The Corner Stone by Margaret Hill McCarter

5.2 Capturing the Text

The next step in republishing *The Corner Stone* was to capture the text. I gently scanned each fragile page of the original book and processed the page images with OCR. As demonstrated earlier, reproducing the text from a book using OCR introduces many errors. In order to minimize mistakes introduced by OCR I tried three different programs to process the page image. One program was designed to translate fax images into text using OCR; another program was designed specifically for OCR in a variety of possible applications; the third program was Microsoft™ OneNote™. In previous experience, the OCR-for-fax program had provided the best results, particularly for poor quality copies. In this case, the error rate was too high and unacceptable. The program purchased specifically for diverse OCR applications also performed poorly. Microsoft™ OneNote™ has an option to make text within an image readable, essentially performing OCR on graphics images; it provided the lowest error rate of the three methods tried. While it was the most accurate method for OCR, it was also the most labor intensive. Obtaining the text for each page required scanning the page, manually selecting the image of the page, selecting the option to make the text in the image readable, and then copying the processed text into another area in OneNote™. This process of capturing all of the text using OCR on scanned images of all of the original 100 pages was surprisingly time consuming.

5.3   Editing the Text, Formatting the Book

The next step in republishing the book was to edit the text -- page by page, line by line, and word by word. One of the biggest challenges was to edit for mistakes – or omissions -- in punctuation and character spacing. As indicated previously, editing the text required nearly as much time as capturing the page images and generating the text using OCR. Having carefully edited the captured text from the original book, I formatted the material to add headers, page numbers, table of contents, and the other elements necessary for a book.

5.4   Preparing an Annotation

Knowing the importance of differentiating a new edition of a previously published book, I researched the author, the time period in which she wrote, and the time period in which the story occurred. I prepared an annotation for the book that contained biographical information on the author and illustrator, historical context for the story, a map of locations mentioned in the story, and a timeline of events in the real world and in the story. Preparing the annotation was motivated by the need to develop a differentiated edition of the book. But as I learned more and more about the author, the illustrator, and events of the day at the time that the story was written, the more intrigued I became. I was glad to have had a chance to get to know Margaret Hill McCarter better, as well as the Kansas of my family history.

5.5 *Reproducing and Restoring Illustrations*

The interior of the original book included a color frontispiece, four black and white pen and ink illustrations, and three unique renderings of a medallion "HE" that was important to the storyline. The pen and ink drawings became my favorites; see Figure 14, for example. I restored them using Photoshop™ to emphasize the contrast, in order to bleach out stains and imperfections from the 100-year old pages. I used the same technique to sharpen the "HE" medallions that appeared throughout the story, Figure 15.

Figure 14 Example of pen and ink illustration from The Corner Stone

Figure 15 Three versions of the "HE" medallion featured in The Corner Stone

5.6 Generating a Cover

The next step in the process of republishing the book was to prepare a cover. I wanted to maintain as much of the original book as I could, so I copied the cover and restored it using Adobe™ Photoshop™. However, the size for new edition was different from the original. I added a border around the original cover image so that I could preserve the scale and illustration of the original but adjust the size to fit the dimensions of the new edition, Figure 16.

Figure 16 Comparison of Original Cover and Restored Cover, The Corner Stone

In addition to the artwork on the cover, I formatted the book to include the frontispiece in the interior pages. With the print options available for low cost publication, it would only be reproduced in black and white. In order to share the original artwork in color with new readers, I used the color image to illustrate the back cover, Figure 17.

Figure 17 Original frontispiece art reproduced on back cover

The final challenge in preparing a cover for the new edition required adapting the font used in the book title on the original cover in order to add "Annotated" to the title of the new edition, Figure 18. Using letters adapted from the original title font made it possible to add "Annotated" unobtrusively to the cover image.

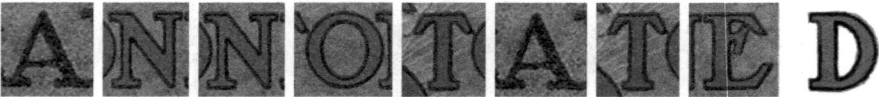

Figure 18 Adapting original font to add "Annotated"

5.7 Case Study Summary

Producing a quality reproduction of *The Corner Stone* was important to me. I am acutely aware that the book is the product of someone else's creativity and effort, not mine. There is merit in republishing books that are otherwise not available so that contemporary readers can enjoy them, but it is important that publishers of public domain works act as responsible stewards of the work. For me, another part of the motivation to produce a quality edition was that this was a book by an early American woman author; not all American women authors have been able to publish their writings widely, and it was important to me that I recognize McCarter's accomplishment. In addition to a sense of obligation to the original author, this was a book that must have been special to my mother, and it described Kansas during a time when my family was settling in the area.

The ultimate measure of merit that I use to assess whether this edition of *The Corner Stone (Annotated)* [26] is worthy of publication is to ask whether seeing it would please Margaret McCarter or her family, whether it would make her proud. I hope so, and I think that is an appropriate measure of merit for other publishers of public domain works.

6   For Readers

Readers who value the creative endeavor that results in a book worth reading can encourage publishers to treat the works of original authors with respect. Ultimately, whether or not a publisher invests in producing high quality editions of public domain works depends on whether they are able to profit from doing so. If readers buy poor quality books from publishers willing to sacrifice accuracy, completeness or quality, those publishers will have no incentive to produce higher quality publications. Here below is a reminder of what readers can do in their own right to ensure quality publications of public domain works that reflect respect for original authors.

6.1   *Do Not Buy Books that Violate Copyright*

While it can be as difficult for a reader to determine copyright status as it is for a publisher – or harder – readers can avoid buying – or downloading -- books from publishers who have not carried out due diligence and are offering copyrighted works for sale as if they are in the public domain. The discussion in *Respect the Work* has for the most part assumed that publishers were acting in good faith, looking to take advantage of works no longer protected by copyright. But the same methods described in these posts to generate new editions of existing works are used by pirates, people who seek to profit from reproduction and distribution of the work of others, irrespective of its copyright status. Or if these groups and individuals are not seeking to make a profit at the expense of the author, at a minimum they disregard the rights of original authors in making books available on sites that provide pirated books, music, videos and other copyrighted materials. As with poor quality editions, rather than obtaining a book from an illegal pirate site, or a copy of a book distributed illegally in violation of copyright, readers can often obtain books legally for free at a site like Project Gutenberg [14]. At Project Gutenberg, out-of-copyright books are being preserved and distributed while protecting legal rights of authors of copyrighted material through exercise of due diligence.

6.2 Let Publishers Know of Poor Quality Editions

Let the publisher know when they have made available a republished edition of a creative work that does not honor the original author. For example, Amazon is committed to a positive reading experience; they encourage readers to identify poor products so that they can inform the publisher of a need to improve. They can and do remove the offending edition from sale, as they did in the case of *Anne of Green Gables*. In order to take action on poor quality books, the publisher needs to know that readers care.

6.3 Do Not Buy "Books" Produced Using Shortcuts

Readers can choose not to buy "books" made up of poor quality images of book pages or books whose text reflects poor editing. If readers buy poor quality republications, publishers have no incentive to invest in providing higher quality editions. For well-known books in the public domain, there may be multiple choices available for purchase; readers can review the options, "Click to Look Inside!' to see the quality of reproduction used by the publisher, look for annotations or other additional context, and choose to buy an edition that offers an appropriate balance of quality reproduction and cost. If a quality edition is not available, rather than paying a publisher for a poor quality reproduction, readers can evaluate options at sites like Project Gutenberg [14] who use volunteers to digitize and proofread their collection of public domain works.

6.4 Buy from Publishers Who Honor Original Authors

Finally, readers can honor the authors of original works by buying from publishers who invest in quality preparation and presentation of works they make available by republication. Let publishers know that it is worth their investment to produce quality publications that reflect appreciation and respect for the creator of the original work.

7 References

1. Amazon.com Inc. *Kindle Direct Publishing*. 2013; Available from: https://kdp.amazon.com.
2. Amazon.com Inc. *CreateSpace*. 2013; Available from: https://www.createspace.com/.
3. Montgomery, L.M. *Anne of Green Gables Deluxe Collection*. 2009 [cited 2013; Available from: http://www.amazon.com/COLLECTION-Annotated-Illustrated-Avonlea-ebook/dp/B00B9I1GUK.
4. Montgomery, L.M. *Anne of Green Gables Collection*. 2012 [cited 2013; Available from: http://www.amazon.com/Anne-Green-Gables-Collection-ebook/dp/B007Q4DC4O.
5. Montgomery, L.M. *Anne of Green Gables (Modern Library Classics)*. 2008 [cited 2013; Available from: http://www.amazon.com/Green-Gables-Modern-Library-Classics/dp/0812979036.
6. Montgomery, L.M. *Anne of Green Gables*. 2013 [cited 2013; Available from: http://www.amazon.com/Anne-of-Green-Gables-ebook/dp/B00BAVHAVA.
7. Montgomery, L.M. *Works of L. M. Montgomery - Complete Anne of Green Gables (Illustrated)*. 2012 [cited 2013; Available from: http://www.amazon.com/Works-L-Montgomery-Illustrated-ebook/dp/B00AGIMYXW.
8. Alija, *Amish Woman*, in *Amish Lifestyle*2010, iStockphoto.
9. Montgomery, L.M. *Anne of Green Gables*. 2012 [cited 2013; Available from: http://www.amazon.com/Anne-Green-Gables-Lucy-Montgomery/dp/1613823762.
10. *The Anne Stories: 12 Books etc.* 2013; Available from: http://www.amazon.com/The-Anne-Stories-Chronicles-ebook/dp/B00BBIT1BO/.

11. Montgomery, L.M. *Anne of Green Gables : Three in One Set : Anne of Green Gables, Anne of Avonlea, Anne of The Island* 2007 [cited 2013; Available from: http://www.amazon.com/Anne-Green-Gables-Avonlea-Island/dp/1481024116.

12. Flood, A., *Anne of Green Gables goes blonde, sparking red hair scare*, in *The Guardian*2013, Guardian News and Media Limited

13. *Product Reviews: "Anne of Green Gables: Three in One Set: Anne of Green Gables, Anne of Avonlea, Anne of The Island"*. 2013 Feb 22, 2013; Available from: http://www.amazon.com/Anne-Green-Gables-Avonlea-Island/product-reviews/1481024116/ref=cm_cr_pr_hist_2?ie=UTF8&filterBy=addTwoStar&showViewpoints=0.

14. *Project Gutenberg.* 2013; Available from: http://www.gutenberg.org.

15. McCarter, M.H., *The Corner Stone*, Forgotten Books.

16. United States Copyright Office. *United States Copyright Office.* 2013 Feb 27, 2013; Available from: http://www.copyright.gov/.

17. Cornell University. *Copyright Information Center.* 2009; Available from: http://copyright.cornell.edu.

18. Hirtle, P.B. *Copyright Term and the Public Domain in the United States.* 2013 Jan 3, 2013; Available from: http://copyright.cornell.edu/resources/publicdomain.cfm.

19. *Copyright Renewal Database*, Stanford University: Stanford, California.

20. Department of Justice. *Justice Laws Website.* 2013 Mar 1, 2013; Available from: http://laws-lois.justice.gc.ca/eng/acts/C-42/index.html.

21. *Long Record: Anne of Windy Poplars*, 2013, Stanford University,: Stanford, California.

22. *Warning! Restricted Access!* ; Available from: http://onlinebooks.library.upenn.edu/webbin/nonus?id=olbp23980.

23. *Amazon Kindle Conditions of Use.* 2013; Available from: https://kindle.amazon.com/conditions_of_use.

24. Montgomery, L.M. *Anne of Green Gables*. 1908 [cited 2013; Available from: http://www.forgottenbooks.org/info/Anne_of_Green_Gables_1000915502.php.

25. Evett, L. and D. Brown, *Text formats and web design for visually impaired and dyslexic readers—Clear Text for All.* Interacting with Computers, 2005. **17**(4): p. 453-472.

26. McCarter, M.H. *The Corner Stone (Annotated).* 2012; Available from: http://www.amazon.com/Corner-Stone-Annotated-Margaret-McCarter/dp/0985665319.

www.ingramcontent.com/pod-product-compliance
Lightning Source LLC
Chambersburg PA
CBHW060632030426
42337CB00018B/3323